Images of God

FOR YOUNG CHILDREN

Marie-Hélène Delval • Barbara Nascimbeni

Images of God

FOR YOUNG CHILDREN

Eerdmans Books for Young Readers

Grand Rapids, Michigan ✢ Cambridge, U.K.

Bl. Eerd. $\frac{1}{11}$ 16.50

Even though we cannot see or touch God, the Bible does describe many ways that we can still discover God in our world. This volume offers a collection of these images, presented here in language that is appropriate for children while remaining faithful to the spirit of the biblical texts.

God is breath.

God is the strong wind
that shapes the earth and sea
and makes the stars shine
to the farthest edge of the heavens.
God is the breath of all living creatures,
the breeze that stirs their hearts,
that refreshes their souls
and renews their spirits.

God is light.

God is light so dazzling
that our eyes cannot look at it.
But the beauty of each day,
the rays of the sun,
the kindness and the joy that light up a face,
the hope and the happiness
that brighten our days —
all these reflect a little of God's light.

God is night.

Night can be scary sometimes,
because you can't see anything,
and because you can lose your way.
Night requires you to be patient
and to wait, believing
that the day will always come again.

God is the word.

Because God speaks to us,
we can hear the words of love
that he whispers
even in the silence.
Because God speaks,
we are able to speak with him.

peace
secret
tears
mercy
bread
breath
wisdom
joy
path
night
strength
promise
wind
love
life

God is silence.

Being quiet is necessary
to understand the cries
of love and of anger,
the millions of questions and complaints,
the secrets and prayers,
that rise up from the earth.

God is secret.

It would be wonderful to know
everything about God —
to discover where he is and what he looks like.
We want to know everything immediately!
But God remains secret for now.
God has his own time.
But that doesn't matter,
because we have our whole lives
to come closer to this great secret.

God is our tears.

If he weren't,
how would he
understand our tears?
How would he cry when we cry?
But God has promised that one day
he will wipe away all the tears
from every eye,
and sadness will no longer exist.

God is joy.

All that God created comes from this joy.
The thousands of beautiful sights on the earth,
the millions of living creatures,
the great whirl of stars in the heavens —
these are an echo of his laughter.
And when our hearts celebrate,
we share in God's laughter and joy.

God is a spring.

No one can live without water.
As our bodies are thirsty for water,
our souls are thirsty for love —
and for beauty and for goodness,
for justice and for truth.
God is all of these and more.
He is the source of all these things,
and he invites us to drink from this spring.

God is a rock.

Rocks are hard. They are solid.
They support anything
that is built on them —
a house, a strong castle.
You can stay standing on a rock
without ever fearing that you will sink down.

God is a stream.

Like a stream that tumbles
joyously down the mountain,
like the blood that flows in our veins,
the flood of God's love
satisfies our thirst
to love and to be loved.

God is the root.

In God, we hold the earth
and touch the heavens.
Through God, we draw in the sap of life
so that our souls bloom
with unseen light.

God is wind.

The wind is free; it blows where it wants.
So does the spirit of God.
The wind sweeps up seeds
that are waiting to sprout wherever they fall,
all over the earth.
In the same way, God sows his word
in the heart of each person.

God is a path.

When everything looks too difficult,
when we don't know where to go anymore,
when it seems we stand before a closed gate
or on the bank of a river
that is impossible to cross,
we need to call on God to help us go forward.
When we understand that his love awaits us,
we won't be mistaken about the path.

God is fire.

When we open up our hearts
and our lives to God,
we receive a fire that gives light and warmth,
but also a fire that burns.
And that can be a little scary.
But God's fire doesn't destroy anything
except what is bad, failed, broken, rotten.
It is a good fire, with a flame that purifies us.

God is a fortress.

Everyone who takes shelter in God
is able to resist attacks
from those who do wrong and bring fear.
God protects them day after day
behind the fortress of his love.

God is a promise.

Because of this, we can be sure
that life is stronger than death,
and that love is stronger than hate.
Because of God, we can believe
that goodness will one day fill the earth,
and that there will no longer be any wickedness,
because he has promised this.
And we can help make this promise
come true a little each day.

God is strength.

There is no love stronger than his,
no gentleness or tenderness
more powerful than God's!
All that God has given us —
forgiveness, life, joy —
comes from his great strength.
And yet, he does so with such gentleness
that no one is forced to accept.

God is wisdom.

Sometimes what happens on earth seems crazy!
People kill, wound, and imprison other people;
they destroy the animals and ruin the planet.
And yet, the earth and the heavens
are so beautiful!
People are beautiful when they work together
to make life good for one another.
Then they bear the image of God,
who created the world with his wisdom.

God is deliverance.

God can deliver us
when we are locked up
by things that keep us from being
loving and joyful and generous,
by everything that prevents us
from looking at life with confidence.

God is a covenant.

When couples give each other rings,
it is a sign that they want to be linked
all the days of their lives.
There is a beautiful story that tells how,
long ago, God gave the ring of a rainbow
to his beloved people,
promising that he would be with them,
now and always.

God is a mystery.

God is present everywhere,
and yet some say that he is not there.
He reigns over the world with his love,
and yet the world is full of misery.
He wants us to know him,
and yet he doesn't show himself.
He is completely unlike us,
and yet he makes us in his image.
But because God is a mystery,
we have to work to understand him better.

God is beauty.

The mountain peaks
and the great depths of the sea,
the light of day and the shadows of night,
the marvelous birds and the fabulous fish,
the multitudes of trees, of plants, and of animals —
all these splendors are just a tiny reflection
of the perfect beauty of God.
But perhaps what reflects God's beauty the best
is the expression of people who love,
who hope, and who work to make life beautiful.

God is justice.

Before judging others, we should see, know,
and understand who they are,
and why they did or did not do something.
We should "walk a mile in their shoes,"
as the proverb says.
God sees, knows, and understands —
much better than we do — exactly who we are,
and why we act the way we do.
God walks in our shoes every day.

God is holiness.

God is perfect beauty,
perfect goodness,
all love, all joy, all peace.
God wants us to have this holiness too.

God is peace.

There are so many people
and so many countries at war!
And some even say
that they fight in the name of God.
God looks all over the earth
for places where his peace can exist.
Let's help him find these places!

God is mercy.

God comforts us when we are not proud
of what we've done.
God always looks at us
with eyes full of mercy,
because he loves in us
what we wish to be.
And under that look of mercy,
we become better.

God is love.

God is love, and love is
patient and considerate.
It is not jealous; it is not proud.
Love is not angry; it forgives everything.
Love lasts forever.

God is a shepherd.

A shepherd always walks near his sheep
to encourage them.
He counts them to make sure
that not a single one has strayed.
He takes them to graze
in the best grassy meadows
so that they will give the best milk.
Like a shepherd, God wants to lead us
where life is the best
so that we can give the best of ourselves.

God is a king.

God is the greatest king of all.
He reigns over the world for eternity.
He is the most magnificent king,
dressed in the splendor of the universe.
God is also the most hidden of kings —
the most secret, the most silent.
He has entrusted the earth to us,
and asks us to reign over it with
care, justice, and goodness.

God is a healer.

God sees what is good in us.
He also sees what is sick.
If we ask him, he will take care of us.
God helps us remove what is bad,
clean what is dirty,
and straighten what is twisted.
As a doctor heals our bodies,
God can heal our hearts.

God is a friend.

You can tell everything to a friend.
You can also be silent around a friend
and simply feel comfortable.
A friend finds the words to comfort you
when you are sad,
and laughs with you when you are happy.
A friend listens, encourages, and understands.
God is like this — like the best of friends.

God is a savior.

When we are about to fall,
when we are sad or frightened,
we need someone to take our hand,
to comfort us and reassure us.
God wants to do that for us.
Sometimes this is difficult to believe.
But if there is still
so much evil, death, and grief in our world,
it is only because
God has not had the last word yet.

God is majesty.

God is everywhere,
and he holds all things:
the earth, the heavens,
and the creatures that live in them.
His glory is even grander than the heavens.
When we try to imagine such greatness,
it can be a little scary,
but we can also just be amazed.

God is smallness.

We know that God is huge.
And yet he also makes himself small.
He decided to live in our world,
to be a baby who needs a mother,
who has to learn to walk and talk.
God is a child
that each one of us
can carry in our arms.

God has a face.

No one has seen God.
But Jesus came to us.
He was born and grew up,
living on earth like all of us.
Jesus told us that God is his father
and our father.
In Jesus, God took on a body and a face.
Those who saw him and touched him
have told us about him.

God is a parent.

A parent says to a child,
"Come, I will show you the world!
Come, I will teach you about life!"
When the child has grown up, the parent says,
"Go on — it's up to you to make your own way!"
The parent watches the child leave,
happy and proud
to see the child walk alone, free.
But the parent still loves the child.
Always!

God is bread.

We need to eat
to live, to grow, and to be strong.
Bread is a symbol of everything that gives life,
of everything that nourishes the earth's people.
If we do not have anything to eat, we die.
God wants us to live.
He has given us Jesus,
and Jesus, in giving us the bread of his body,
gives us never-ending life from God.

God *is* life.

We know how seeds sprout and grow
to become plants and trees.
We know how a baby forms
month by month in a mother's belly.
But the spark of life —
where does that come from?
That is the great mystery!
If God is the one who gives life,
then God *is* life.

God is with us.

This God of words and of silence,
this God of light and of night,
this God who is strength, beauty, peace,
love, and forgiveness,
this God who heals, who frees,
and who saves —
this God is the one we call "Our Father."
He is with us every day,
until the day we will be with him.

Other books in this series:

Psalms for Young Children
Marie-Hélène Delval • Arno

The Bible for Young Children
Marie-Hélène Delval • Götting

Animals of the Bible for Young Children
Marie-Hélène Delval • Aurélia Fronty

© 2010 Bayard Éditions Jeunesse as *Les Visages de Dieu pour les tout-petits*

This edition published in 2011 by
Eerdmans Books for Young Readers,
an imprint of William B. Eerdmans Publishing Co.
2140 Oak Industrial Dr. NE, Grand Rapids, Michigan 49505
P.O. Box 163, Cambridge CB3 9PU U.K.

www.eerdmans.com/youngreaders

Manufactured at Toppan Leefung Printing Ltd in Guangdong Province, China, September 2010, first printing

11 12 13 14 15 16 17   10 9 8 7 6 5 4 3 2 1

Library of Congress Cataloging-in-Publication Data

Delval, Marie-Hélène.
[Visages de Dieu. English]
Images of God for young children / written by Marie-Hélène Delval; illustrated by Barbara Nascimbeni.
p. cm.
ISBN 978-0-8028-5391-2 (alk. paper)
1. God (Christianity) — Juvenile literature. I. Nascimbeni, Barbara, ill. II. Title.
BT107.D4813 2011
231 — dc22
2010025534